U.S. NAVY

by Jill Sherman

AMICUS | AMICUS INK

Amicus High Interest is published by Amicus and Amicus Ink
P.O. Box 1329, Mankato, MN 56002
www.amicuspublishing.us

Names: Sherman, Jill, author.
Title: U.S. Navy / by Jill Sherman.
Description: Mankato, Minnesota : Amicus, [2019] | Series: Serving our country | Includes index. | Audience: Grades K-3.
Identifiers: LCCN 2018002417 (print) | LCCN 2018002884 (ebook) | ISBN 9781681516028 (pdf) | ISBN 9781681515649 (library binding) | ISBN 9781681524023 (pbk.)
Subjects: LCSH: United States. Navy--Juvenile literature
Classification: LCC VA58.4 (ebook) | LCC VA58.4 .S53 2019 (print) | DDC 359.00973--dc23
LC record available at https://lccn.loc.gov/2018002417

Photo Credits: Shutterstock/Nikola m background pattern; DVIDS/U.S. Navy/Mass Communication Specialist 3rd Class Robyn B. Melvin cover, Mass Communication Specialist 2nd Class Ryan U. Kledzik 2, Seaman Apprentice Carla Ocampo 4, Mass Communication Specialist 3rd Class Sarah Myers 6–7, General Dynamics Electric Boat 21, Mass Communication Specialist 3rd Class Colbey Livingston 22; Flickr/U.S. Navy photo 8–9, Mass Communication Specialist 3rd Class Dylan

McCord 11, Erik Hildebrandt 12–13, Mass Communication Specialist 2nd Class Alan Gragg 18; Wiki Commons/U.S. Navy photo/Released 14–15; Navy.mil/U.S. Navy photo by Chief Mass Communication Specialist Dean Lohmeyer 17

Editor: Wendy Dieker
Designer: Aubrey Harper
Photo Researcher: Holly Young

Printed in China

HC 10 9 8 7 6 5 4 3 2 1
PB 10 9 8 7 6 5 4 3 2 1

TABLE OF CONTENTS

ON THE HIGH SEAS

Who protects our country's water? The U.S. Navy does. The sailors sail along the shore. They sail across the ocean. They keep America's ships and shores safe.

Force Fact
George Washington formed our country's first navy in 1775.

NAVY SHIPS

The United States has the largest navy in the world. There are more than 270 ships. Some ships are armed with weapons. The biggest ships carry planes. The smallest ships patrol the seas.

8

WARSHIPS

War breaks out. Enemy ships are sailing across the ocean. The Navy sends sailors. They are on a **missile cruiser**. They fire missiles at the enemy ships.

A FLOATING CITY

The Navy wants to stay close to the action. They send an **aircraft carrier**. It is like a floating city. It even has an **airstrip**. Hundreds of sailors and pilots live on the ocean for months.

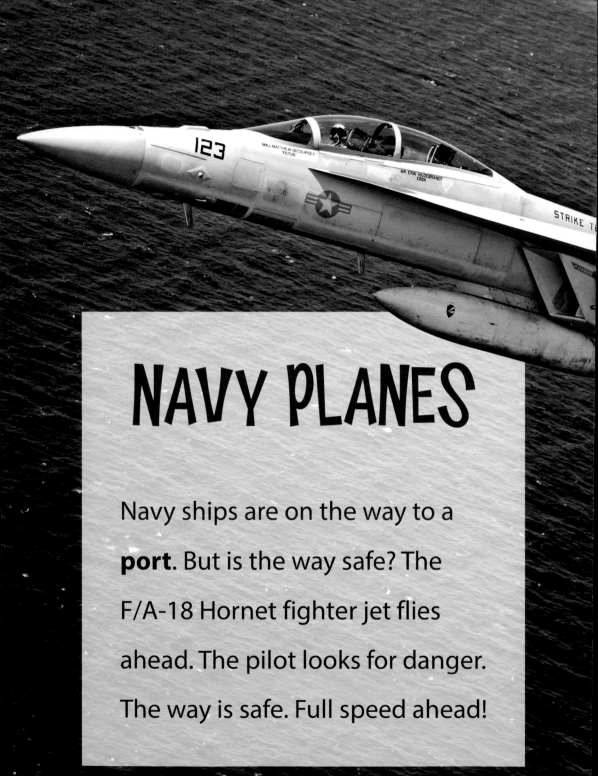

NAVY PLANES

Navy ships are on the way to a **port**. But is the way safe? The F/A-18 Hornet fighter jet flies ahead. The pilot looks for danger. The way is safe. Full speed ahead!

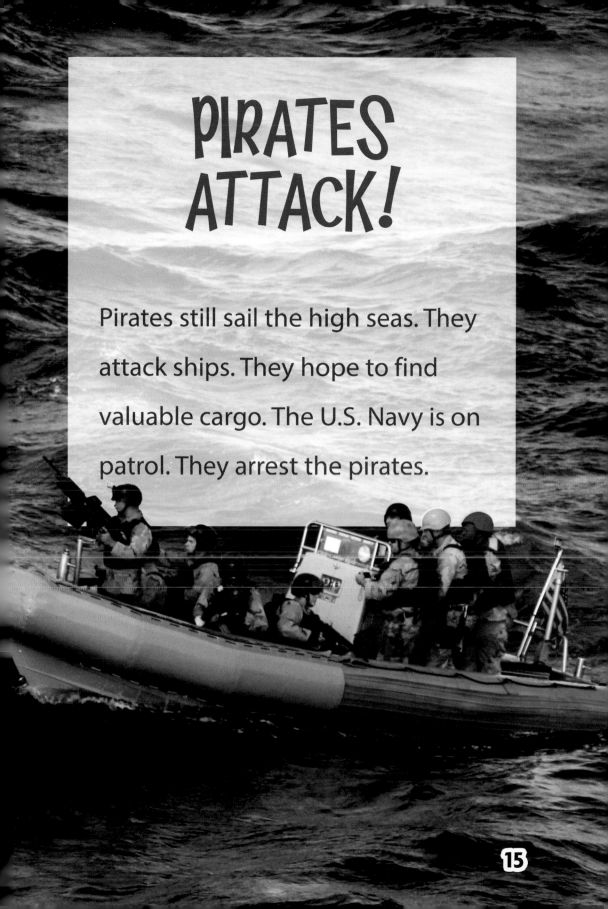

PIRATES ATTACK!

Pirates still sail the high seas. They attack ships. They hope to find valuable cargo. The U.S. Navy is on patrol. They arrest the pirates.

UNDER THE SEA

A submarine quietly roams deep in the ocean. It is 560 feet (171 m) long. But it has **stealth technology**. Enemies can't see it. From below the water, the sub fires. It's a hit! The enemy ship sinks.

Force Fact
Sub crews stay underwater for months at a time.

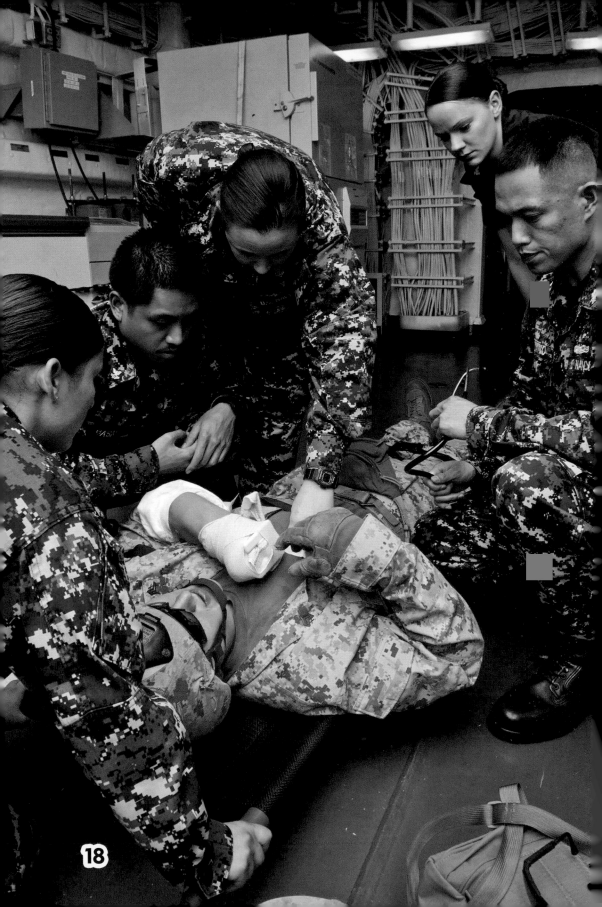

TO THE RESCUE!

A Navy ship was attacked! It is damaged. Sailors are hurt. **Support ships** come to the rescue. A hospital ship is sent. A tugboat comes to pull the ship to port.

FULL SPEED AHEAD

The U.S. Navy is ready for action. They work on ships. They dive deep in subs. They even fly high in planes. Every day, the brave men and women of the U.S. Navy keep us safe.

U.S. NAVY FAST FACTS

Founded: 1775

Members called: Sailors

Main duties: To protect the nation's ships and shore

Members on active duty: 323,850

Motto: "Semper fortis" (Always courageous)

WORDS TO KNOW

aircraft carrier A very large ship that carries planes and helicopters; the deck is a runway for planes to take off from and land on.

airstrip A runway where planes can take off and land.

missile cruiser A fast ship that is armed with missiles that can fire at enemies.

port A place on shore set up for boats to land.

stealth technology Features and design that makes the boat or plane hard to find on radar.

support ship A ship that helps other vehicles at sea; support ships might bring fuel, help pull a damaged ship to land, or bring medical aid.

LEARN MORE

Books

Boothroyd, Jennifer. *Inside the US Navy*. Minneapolis: Lerner Books, 2017.

Grack, Rachel. *U.S. Special Forces*. Mankato, Minn.: Amicus, 2019.

Marx, Mandy. *Amazing US Navy Facts*. Mankato, Minn.: Capstone Publishers, 2017.

Websites

America's Navy Recruiting: Navy.com
www.navy.com

National Museum of the US Navy
www.history.navy.mil/content/history/museums/nmusn.html

INDEX